THE NEW DECADE SERIES

PIANO • VOCAL • GUITAR

MW00654740

SONGS OF THE 1950s

100 Songs with Online Audio Backing Tracks

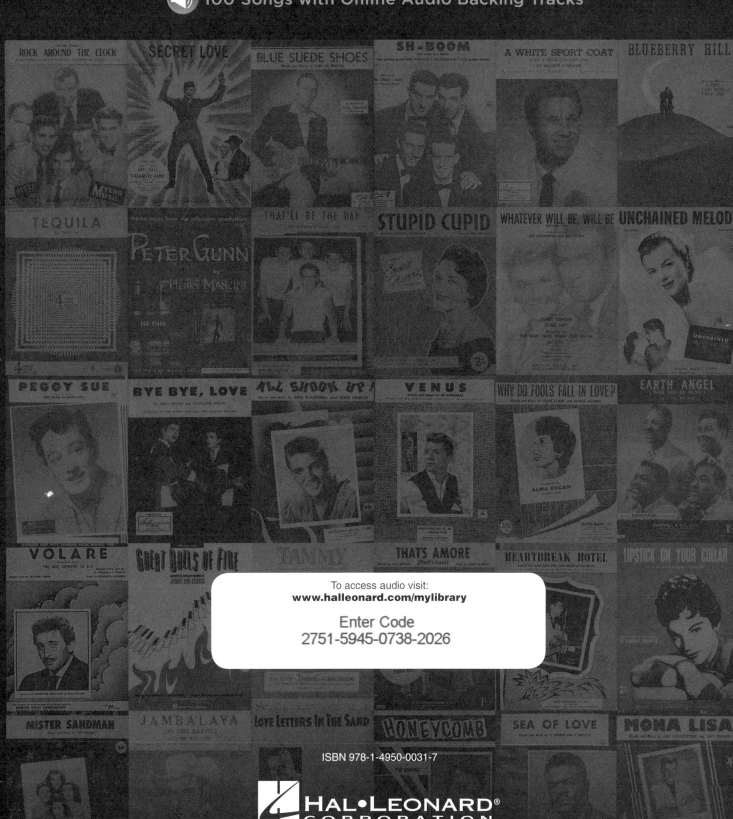

To access audio visit:
www.halleonard.com/mylibrary

Enter Code
2751-5945-0738-2026

ISBN 978-1-4950-0031-7

HAL•LEONARD® CORPORATION

7777 W. BLUEMOUND RD. P.O. BOX 13819 MILWAUKEE, WI 53213

Visit Hal Leonard Online at
www.halleonard.com

AIN'T THAT A SHAME

Words and Music by ANTOINE DOMINO
and DAVE BARTHOLOMEW

ALL I HAVE TO DO IS DREAM

Words and Music by
BOUDLEAUX BRYANT

ALL SHOOK UP

Words and Music by OTIS BLACKWELL
and ELVIS PRESLEY

Medium Shuffle

A - well - a, bless my soul, ___ what's wrong with me? ___ I'm

itch - ing like a man ___ on a fuzz - y tree. ___ My friends say I'm act - in'

queer as a bug, ___ I'm in love! ___ I'm all shook up! ___ Mm ___

AT THE HOP

Words and Music by ARTHUR SINGER,
JOHN MADARA and DAVID WHITE

BLUE SUEDE SHOES

Words and Music by
CARL LEE PERKINS

Brightly, not too fast

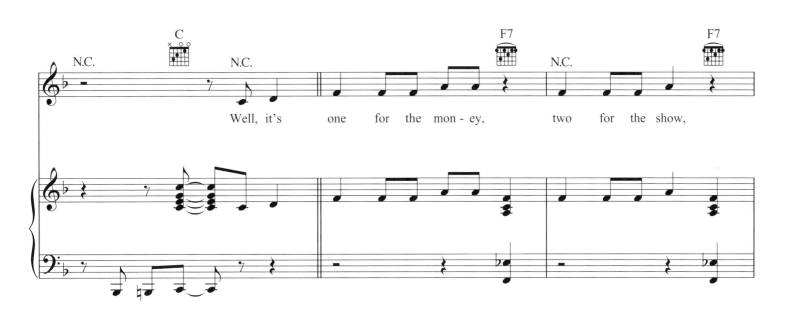

Well, it's one for the mon-ey, two for the show,

three to get read-y, now go, cat, go! But don't you

BE-BOP-A-LULA

Words and Music by TEX DAVIS
and GENE VINCENT

Moderately slow Rock

Be-bop-a-lu - la, she's my ba - by. Be-bop-a-lu - la, I don't mean may - be.

Be-bop-a-lu - la, she's my ba - by. Be-bop-a-lu - la, I don't mean may - be.

Be-bop-a-lu - la, she's my ba - by doll, my ba - by doll, my ba - by doll.

BLUEBERRY HILL

Words and Music by AL LEWIS,
LARRY STOCK and VINCENT ROSE

BYE BYE LOVE

Words and Music by FELICE BRYANT
and BOUDLEAUX BRYANT

BO DIDDLEY

Words and Music by
ELLAS McDANIEL

Brightly, a la Calypso

to make his pret-ty ba-by a Sun-day hat. ___

Won't you come to my house and rack that bone, ___

Take my ba-by all the way from home.

Look at that bo-do, oh,

where's he been? _

Up to your house and gone a - gain.

Bo Did-dl-ey, Bo Did-dl-ey, have you heard? _

Repeat and Fade

My _ pret-ty ba-by said she was a bird.

CANADIAN SUNSET

Words by NORMAN GIMBEL
Music by EDDIE HEYWOOD

CHANCES ARE

Words by AL STILLMAN
Music by ROBERT ALLEN

Moderately, with great warmth

Chanc - es   are   'cause I   wear a sil - ly grin,   the

mo - ment you come in - to view,   chanc - es are you think that

I'm   in   love with   you. _____   Just be - cause   my com-

CHANTILLY LACE

Words and Music by
J.P. RICHARDSON

Moderate Boogie-woogie

(Spoken:) Oh,

you sweet thing!

Do I what?

Will I what?

COLD, COLD HEART

Words and Music by
HANK WILLIAMS

44

COME GO WITH ME

Words and Music by
C.E. QUICK

CRY

Words and Music by
CHURCHILL KOHLMAN

50

DON'T BE CRUEL
(To a Heart That's True)

Words and Music by OTIS BLACKWELL
and ELVIS PRESLEY

Moderately, with a half-time feel

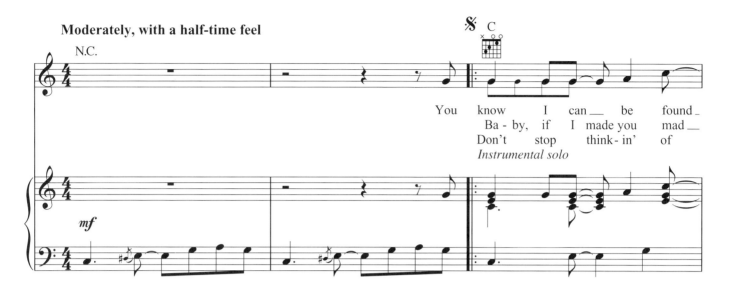

You know I can __ be found __
Ba - by, if I made you mad __
Don't stop think - in' of
Instrumental solo

__ sit - tin' home all a - lone. __ If
for some - thing I might have __ said, __ Come
me. Don't make me feel this __ way.

you can't come _ a - round, at least please tel - e - phone. _
please let's for - get the past. The fu - ture looks bright a - head. _
on o - ver here and love me. You know what I want you to

DIANA

Words and Music by
PAUL ANKA

DREAM LOVER

Words and Music by
BOBBY DARIN

EARTH ANGEL

Words and Music by
JESSE BELVIN

FEVER

Words and Music by JOHN DAVENPORT
and EDDIE COOLEY

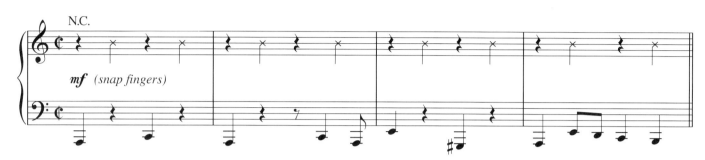

1. Nev - er know how much I love you, nev - er know how much I
2. Sun lights up the day - time, moon lights up the night.
3. Ro - me - o loved Ju - li - et. Ju - li - et, she felt the
4. Cap - tain Smith and Po - ca - hon - tas had a ver - y mad af -
5. Now you've lis - tened to my sto - ry. Here's the point that I have

care. When you put your arms a - round me, I get a
night. I light up when you call my name, and you
same. When he put his arms a - round her, he said,
fair. When her dad - dy tried to kill him, she said,
made. Chicks were born to give you fe - ver, be it

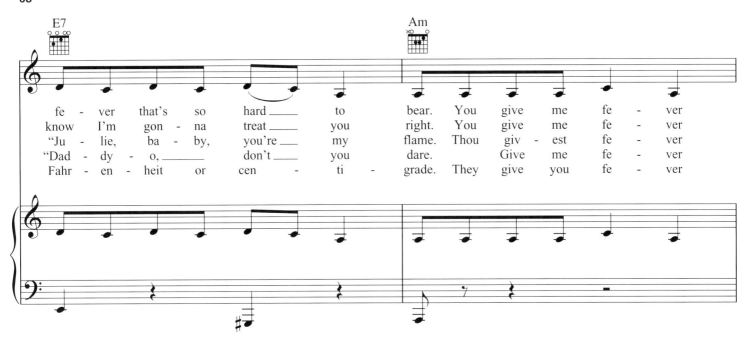

fe - ver that's so hard ___ to bear. You give me fe - ver
know I'm gon - na treat ___ you right. You give me fe - ver
"Ju - lie, ba - by, you're ___ my flame. Thou giv - est fe - ver
"Dad - dy - o, ___ don't ___ you dare. Give me fe - ver
Fahr - en - heit or cen - ti - grade. They give you fe - ver

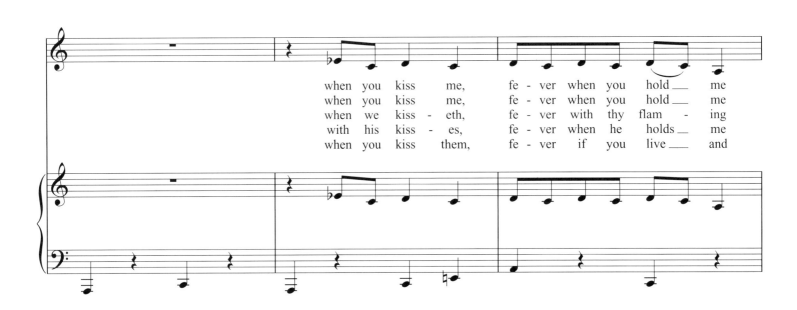

when you kiss me, fe - ver when you hold ___ me
when you kiss me, fe - ver when you hold ___ me
when we kiss - eth, fe - ver with thy flam - ing
with his kiss - es, fe - ver when he holds ___ me
when you kiss them, fe - ver if you live ___ and

tight, fe - ver in the morn - ing,
tight, fe - ver in the morn - ing,
youth. Fe - ver, I'm a - fire. ___
tight. Fe - ver, I'm his mis - sus. Oh,
learn. Fe - ver till you siz - zle,

GREAT BALLS OF FIRE

Words and Music by JACK HAMMER
and OTIS BLACKWELL

Bright Rock

You shake my nerves and you rat-tle my brain. _
Instrumental

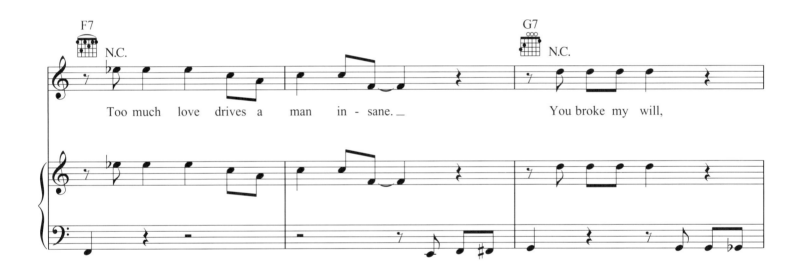

Too much love drives a man in-sane. _   You broke my will,

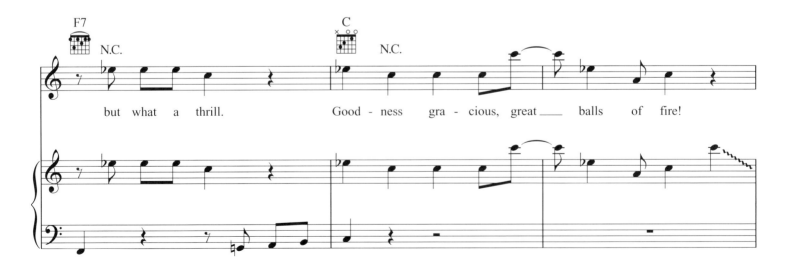

but what a thrill.   Good - ness gra - cious, great ___ balls of fire!

THE GREAT PRETENDER

Words and Music by
BUCK RAM

HEARTBREAK HOTEL

Words and Music by MAE BOREN AXTON,
TOMMY DURDEN and ELVIS PRESLEY

Well, since my __ ba-by left me, well, I've found a new place to dwell. Well, it's

down at the end __ of Lone-ly Street at Heart-break Ho-tel where I'll be, I'll be just so lone-ly, ba-by.

Well, I'm so lone-ly, I'll be just so lone-ly ___ I could die. Al-

Heart - break Ho - tel where you will be, will be just so lone - ly, ba - by,

well, you'll be lone - ly. You'll be so lone - ly ___ you could die.

A9

Piano solo ad lib.

THE GREEN DOOR

Words and Music by BOB DAVIE
and MARVIN MOORE

HONEYCOMB

Words and Music by
BOB MERRILL

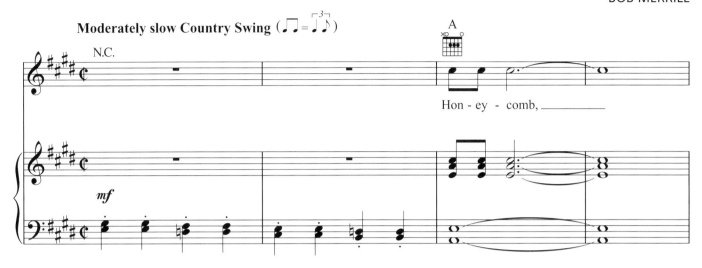

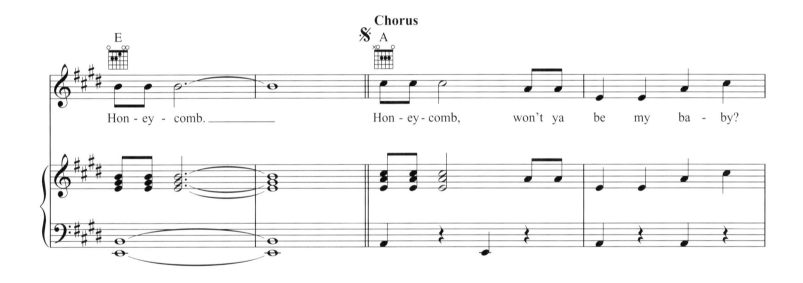

Additional Lyrics

2. Now have you heard tell how they made a bee,
Then tried a hand at a green, green tree?
So the tree was made and I guess you've heard,
Next they made a bird.
Then they went around lookin' everywhere,
Takin' love from here and from there,
And they stored it up in a little cart
For my honey's heart.
Chorus

HOUND DOG

Words and Music by JERRY LEIBER
and MIKE STOLLER

Moderate Shuffle

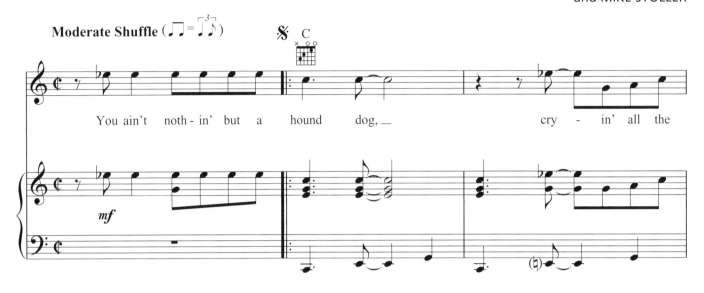

You ain't noth-in' but a hound dog, ___ cry-in' all the

time. You ain't noth-in' but a hound dog, ___

cry-in' all the time. Well, ___ you ain't

I HEAR YOU KNOCKING

Words and Music by DAVE BARTHOLOMEW
and PEARL KING

I WALK THE LINE

Words and Music by
JOHN R. CASH

1. I keep a close watch on this heart of
2. ver - y eas - y to be
3.–5. *(See additional lyrics)*

mine. _____ I keep my eyes wide
true. _____ I find my - self a - lone

o - pen all the time. _____ I keep the
when each day is through. _____ Yes, I'll ad -

Additional Lyrics

3. As sure as night is dark and day is light,
   I keep you on my mind both day and night.
   And happiness I've known proves that it's right.
   Because you're mine I walk the line.

4. You've got a way to keep me on your side.
   You give me cause for love that I can't hide.
   For you I know I'd even try to turn the tide.
   Because you're mine I walk the line.

5. I keep a close watch on this heart of mine.
   I keep my eyes wide open all the time.
   I keep the ends out for the tie that binds.
   Because you're mine I walk the line.

I WANT YOU, I NEED YOU, I LOVE YOU

Words by MAURICE MYSELS
Music by IRA KOSLOFF

IT'S ALL IN THE GAME

Lyrics by CARL SIGMAN
Music by CHARLES GATES DAWES

IT'S ONLY MAKE BELIEVE

Words and Music by CONWAY TWITTY
and JACK NANCE

IT'S SO EASY

Words and Music by BUDDY HOLLY
and NORMAN PETTY

JAILHOUSE ROCK

Words and Music by JERRY LEIBER
and MIKE STOLLER

Additional Lyrics

2. Spider Murphy played the tenor saxophone
   Little Joe was blowin' on the slide trombone.
   The drummer boy from Illinois went crash, boom, bang;
   The whole rhythm section was the Purple Gang.
   Chorus

3. Number forty-seven said to number three
   "You're the cutest jailbird I ever did see.
   I sure would be delighted with your company,
   Come on and do the Jailhouse Rock with me."
   Chorus

4. The sad sack was a-sittin' on a block of stone,
   Way over in the corner weeping all alone.
   The warden said: "Hey, Buddy, don't you be no square,
   If you can't find a partner, use a wooden chair!"
   Chorus

5. Shifty Henry said to Bugs: "For heaven's sake,
   No one's lookin', now's our chance to make a break."
   Bugsy turned to Shifty and he said: "Nix, nix;
   I wanna stick around a while and get my kicks."
   Chorus

JAMBALAYA
(On the Bayou)

Words and Music by
HANK WILLIAMS

KANSAS CITY

Words and Music by JERRY LEIBER
and MIKE STOLLER

LIPSTICK ON YOUR COLLAR

Words by EDNA LEWIS
Music by GEORGE GOEHRING

LITTLE DARLIN'

Words and Music by
MAURICE WILLIAMS

(Spoken over repeat:) *(optional)*

My dear, I need your love to call my own
And never do wrong; and to hold in mine your little hand.
I'll know too soon that I'll love again.
Please come back to me.

LOLLIPOP

Words and Music by BEVERLY ROSS
and JULIUS DIXON

With an easy shuffle

Lol - li - pop, lol - li - pop, oh, ____ lol - li, lol - li, lol - li, lol - li - pop, lol - li - pop, oh, ____ lol - li, lol - li, lol - li, lol - li - pop, lol - li - pop, oh, ____ lol - li - lol - li, lol - li, lol - li - pop.

Call my ba - by lol - li - pop,
Cra - zy way she thrills - a me,

LONELY TEARDROPS

Words and Music by BERRY GORDY,
GWEN GORDY FUQUA and TYRAN CARLO

LOVE LETTERS IN THE SAND

Words by NICK KENNY and CHARLES KENNY
Music by J. FRED COOTS

136

(You've Got)
THE MAGIC TOUCH

Words and Music by
BUCK RAM

Moderately with a light Swing feel

You've got the mag-ic touch. _____ It makes me

glow so much. _____ It casts a spell, _____ it rings a

bell, the mag-ic touch. _____ Oh, when I

LOVE ME

Words and Music by JERRY LEIBER
and MIKE STOLLER

Moderately slow

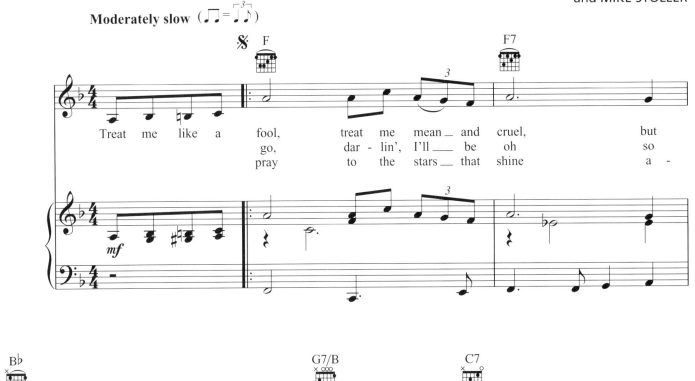

Treat me like a fool, treat me mean and cruel, but
go, dar - lin', I'll __ be oh so
pray to the stars __ that shine a -

love me. ___
lone - ly. ___
bove me, ___

Break my faith - ful heart.   Tear it all a -
I'll be sad and blue,   cry - ing o - ver
beg - ging on my knees   all I ask is

part, ___ but love me. ___   If you ev - er

LOVE ME TENDER

Words and Music by ELVIS PRESLEY
and VERA MATSON

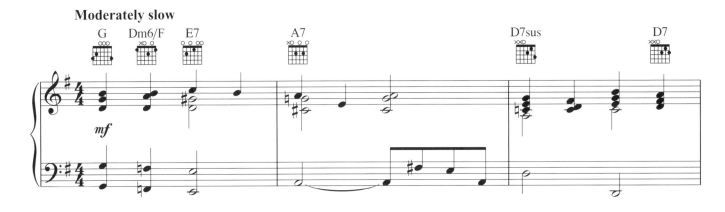

Love me ten - der, love me sweet,
Love me ten - der, love me long,
Love me ten - der, love me dear,
When at last my dreams come true,

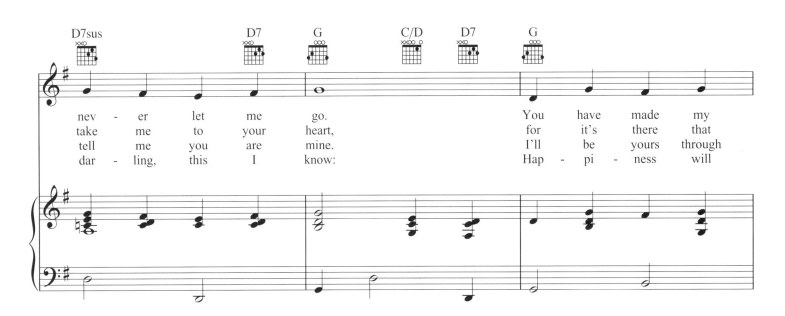

nev - er let me go.
take me to your heart,
tell me you are mine.
dar - ling, this I know:

You have made my
for it's there that
I'll be yours through
Hap - pi - ness will

LOVING YOU

Words and Music by JERRY LEIBER
and MIKE STOLLER

Moderately slow

I will spend my whole life through ___
If I'm seen with some-one new, ___

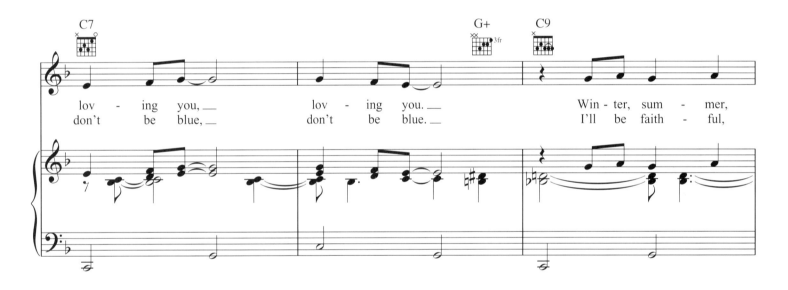

lov-ing you, ___ lov-ing you. ___ Win-ter, sum-mer,
don't be blue, ___ don't be blue. ___ I'll be faith-ful,

spring-time, too, ___ lov-ing you, ___ lov-ing you. ___
I'll be true, ___ al-ways true, ___ true to you. ___

MAYBE BABY

By NORMAN PETTY
and CHARLES HARDIN

MEMORIES ARE MADE OF THIS

Words and Music by RICHARD DEHR,
FRANK MILLER and TERRY GILKYSON

MISTY

Words by JOHNNY BURKE
Music by ERROLL GARNER

MISTER SANDMAN

Words and Music by
PAT BALLARD

MOMENTS TO REMEMBER

Words by AL STILLMAN
Music by ROBERT ALLEN

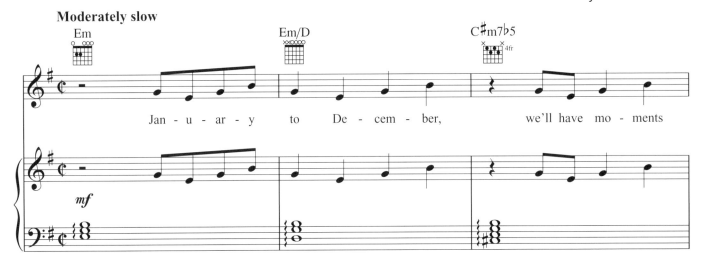

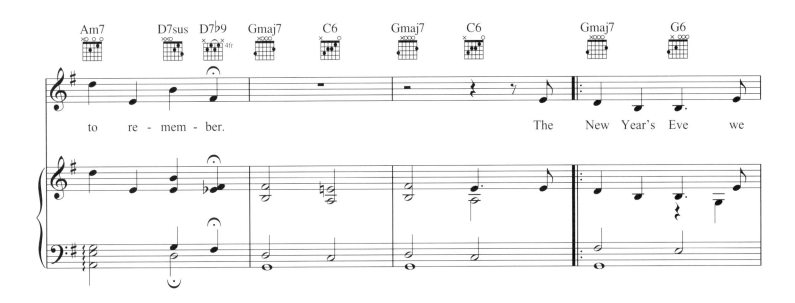

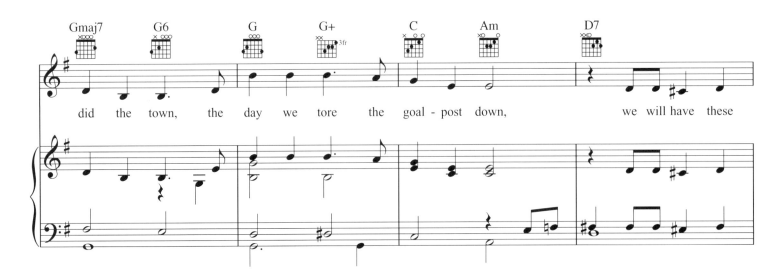

MONA LISA
from the Paramount Picture CAPTAIN CAREY, U.S.A.

Words and Music by JAY LIVINGSTON
and RAY EVANS

MY PRAYER

Music by GEORGES BOULANGER
Lyric and Musical Adaptation by JIMMY KENNEDY

When the twi-light is gone _____ and no song-bird is sing-ing, _____
____ when the twi-light is gone _____ you come in-to my

OH, LONESOME ME

Words and Music by
DON GIBSON

172

PEGGY SUE

Words and Music by JERRY ALLISON,
NORMAN PETTY and BUDDY HOLLY

174

ONLY YOU
(And You Alone)

Words and Music by BUCK RAM
and ANDE RAND

(You've Got)
PERSONALITY

Words and Music by LLOYD PRINCE
and HAROLD LOGAN

PETER GUNN
Theme Song from the Television Series

By HENRY MANCINI

loco

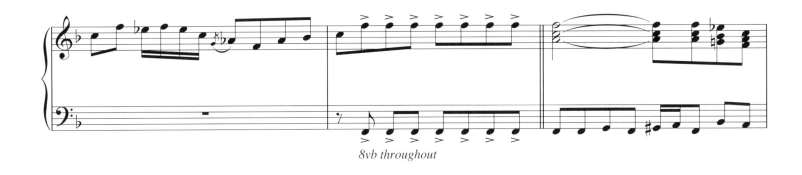

8vb throughout

PUT YOUR HEAD ON MY SHOULDER

Words and Music by
PAUL ANKA

189

QUE SERA, SERA
(Whatever Will Be, Will Be)

Words and Music by JAY LIVINGSTON
and RAYMOND B. EVANS

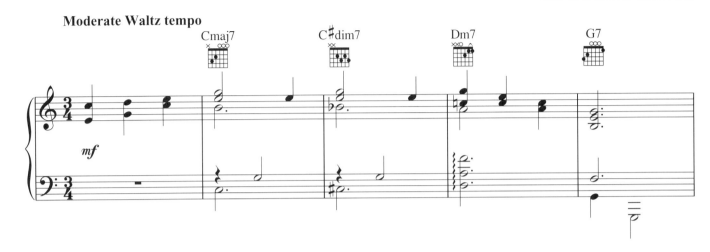

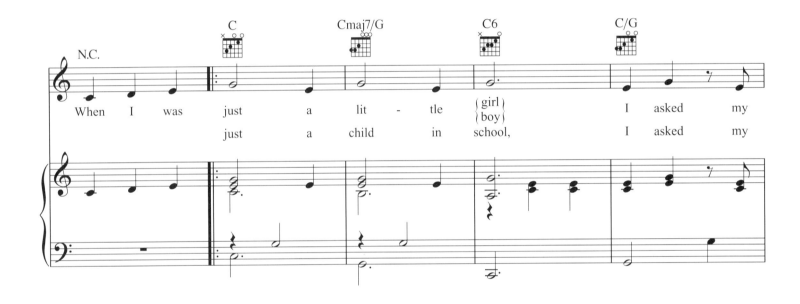

When I was just a lit - tle {girl} {boy}, I asked my
just a child in school, I asked my

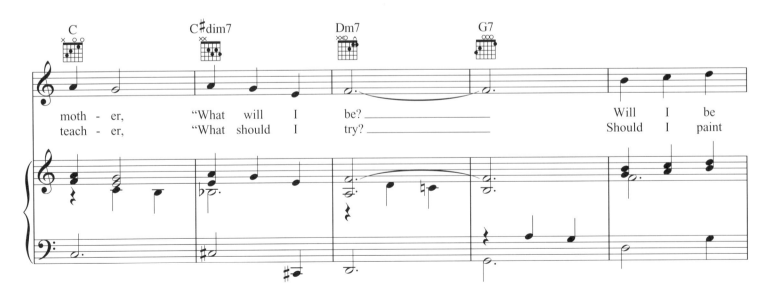

moth - er, "What will I be? _____ Will I be
teach - er, "What should I try? _____ Should I be paint

ROCK AROUND THE CLOCK

Words and Music by MAX C. FREEDMAN
and JIMMY DeKNIGHT

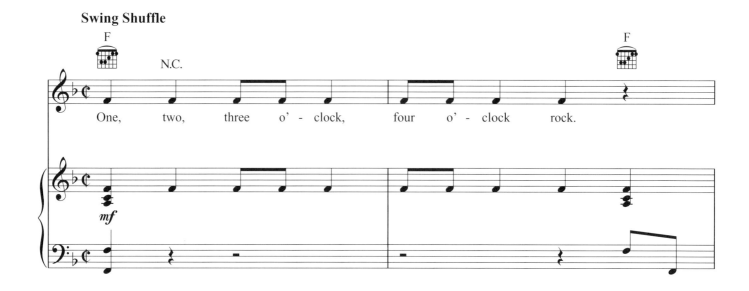

One, two, three o'-clock, four o'-clock rock.

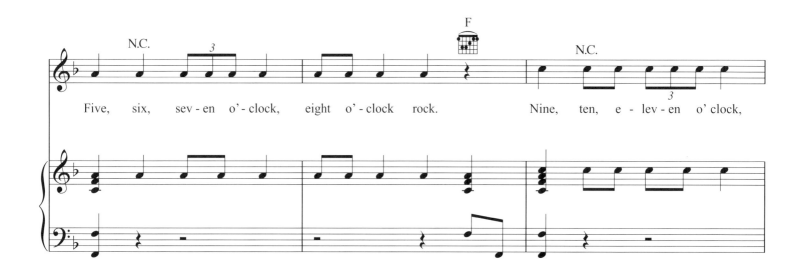

Five, six, sev-en o'-clock, eight o'-clock rock. Nine, ten, e-lev-en o'-clock,

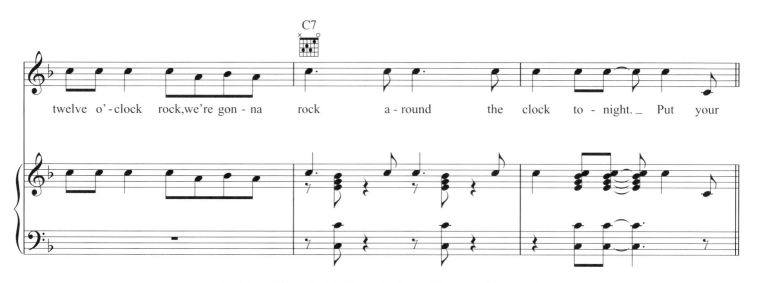

twelve o'-clock rock, we're gon-na rock a-round the clock to-night.__ Put your

SEA OF LOVE

Words and Music by GEORGE KHOURY
and PHILIP BAPTISTE

SEARCHIN'

Words and Music by JERRY LEIBER
and MIKE STOLLER

Not too fast, with a strong afterbeat

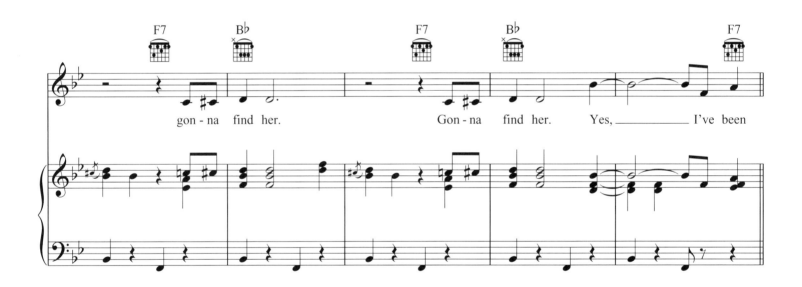

SECRET LOVE

Words by PAUL FRANCIS WEBSTER
Music by SAMMY FAIN

SEE YOU LATER, ALLIGATOR

Words and Music by
ROBERT GUIDRY

Well, I saw my ba-by walk-ing with an-oth-er man to-
told me, near-ly made me lose my
dad-dy, you know my love is just for
'ga-tor, I know you meant it just for

day; ___ well, I saw my ba-by walk-ing
head; ___ when I thought of what she told me,
you." ___ She said, "I'm sor-ry, pret-ty dad-dy,
play." ___ I said,"Wait a min-ute, 'ga-tor,

with an - oth - er man to - day. ___
near - ly made me lose my head. ___
you know my love is just for you. ___
I know you meant it just for play." _

When I asked her what's the
But the next time that I
Won't you say that you'll for -
Don't you know you real - ly

mat - ter,
saw her,
give me,
hurt me,

this is what I heard her say:
re - mind - ed her of what she said.
and say your love for me is true?"
and this is what I have to say:

"See you lat - er, al - li - ga - tor,

af - ter 'while, ___ croc - o -

SHAKE, RATTLE AND ROLL

Words and Music by
CHARLES CALHOUN

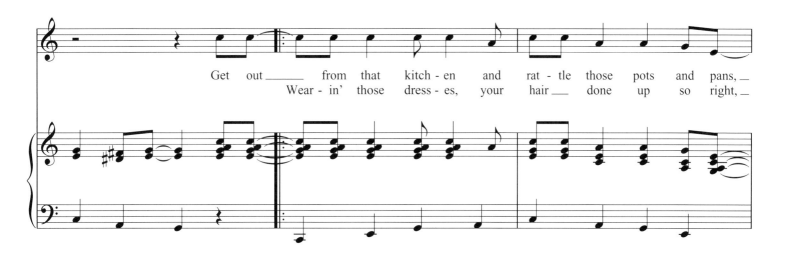

Get out ___ from that kitch-en and rat-tle those pots and pans, ___
Wear-in' those dress-es, your hair ___ done up so right, ___

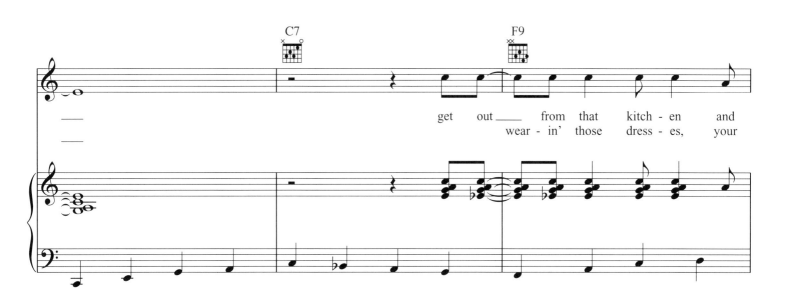

___ get out ___ from that kitch-en and
___ wear-in' those dress-es, your

SH-BOOM

Words and Music by JAMES KEYES,
CLAUDE FEASTER, CARL FEASTER,
FLOYD McRAE and JAMES EDWARDS

SHOUT

Words and Music by O'KELLY ISLEY,
RONALD ISLEY and RUDOLPH ISLEY

222

SINCE I DON'T HAVE YOU

Words and Music by JAMES BEAUMONT,
JANET VOGEL, JOSEPH VERSCHAREN,
WALTER LESTER, LENNIE MARTIN,
JOSEPH ROCK and JOHN TAYLOR

SINCERELY

Words and Music by ALAN FREED
and HARVEY FUQUA

Slowly, with a good beat

Sin - cere - ly, _____ oh! _ Yes, _ sin - cere - ly,

'cause I love you so _ dear - ly, _____ please say _ you'll be

mine. _____ Sin - cere - ly, _____

SINCE I MET YOU BABY

Words and Music by
IVORY JOE HUNTER

Since I met you, ba - by, my whole life has changed. ___
Since I met you, ba - by, I'm a hap - py man. ___

Since I met you, ba - by, my whole life has changed. ___
Since I met you, ba - by, I'm a hap - py man. ___

And ev - 'ry - bod - y tells me that I am not the
I'm gon - na try to please you in ev - 'ry way I

SINGING THE BLUES

Words and Music by
MELVIN ENDSLEY

241

SIXTEEN CANDLES

Words and Music by LUTHER DIXON
and ALLYSON R. KHENT

SIXTEEN TONS

Words and Music by
MERLE TRAVIS

Moderately, with a slight lilt

Some peo-ple say a man is made out of mud. ___ A
born ___ one ___ morn-in' when the sun did-n't shine. ___ I
born ___ one ___ morn-in', it was driz-zl-ing rain, _____
see ___ me ___ com-in', bet-ter step a-side. ___ A

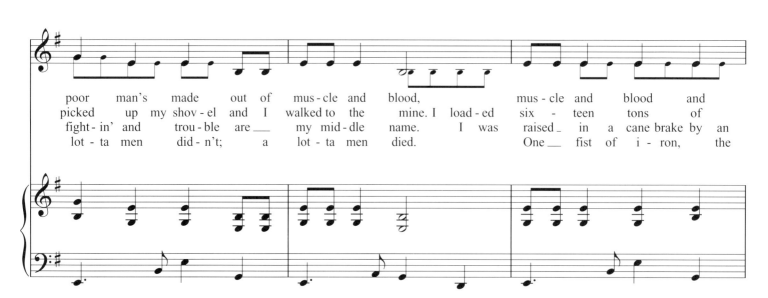

poor man's made out of mus-cle and blood, mus-cle and blood and
picked up my shov-el and I walked to the mine. I load-ed six-teen tons of
fight-in' and trou-ble are ___ my mid-dle name. I was raised ___ in a cane brake by an
lot-ta men did-n't; a lot-ta men died. One ___ fist of i-ron, the

SPLISH SPLASH

Words and Music by BOBBY DARIN
and MURRAY KAUFMAN

STAGGER LEE

Words and Music by LLOYD PRICE
and HAROLD LOGAN

The night was clear and the moon was yel-low, __ and the leaves came tum-bling down.

I was stand-ing __ on the cor-ner __ when I
Lee __ told Bil-ly, __ "I can't
Lee __ went to the bar-room, __ and he

heard my bull-dog bark. He was bark-ing at the two men who were
let you go with that. You have won all my __ mon-ey and my
stood a-cross the bar-room door. Said, "Now no-bod-y move," and he

STUPID CUPID

Words and Music by HOWARD GREENFIELD
and NEIL SEDAKA

SUMMERTIME BLUES

Words and Music by EDDIE COCHRAN
and JERRY CAPEHART

Some-times I won-der what I'm a-gon-na do, ___ but there ain't no cure for the

sum - mer - time ___ blues.

Play 3 times

(Let Me Be Your)
TEDDY BEAR

Words and Music by KAL MANN
and BERNIE LOWE

263

TAMMY

Words and Music by JAY LIVINGSTON
and RAY EVANS

A TEENAGER IN LOVE

Words by DOC POMUS
Music by MORT SHUMAN

Each time we have a quar-rel it al-most breaks my heart,
One day I feel so hap-py; next day I feel so sad.

'cause I am so a-fraid that we will have to part.
I guess I'll so learn to take the good with the bad.

Each night I ask the stars up a-bove:

TEQUILA

By CHUCK RIO

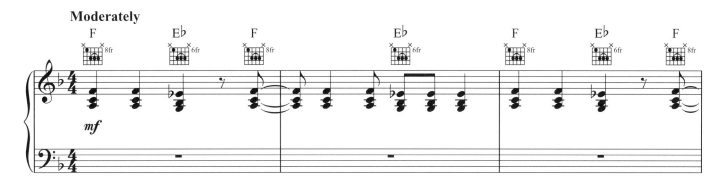

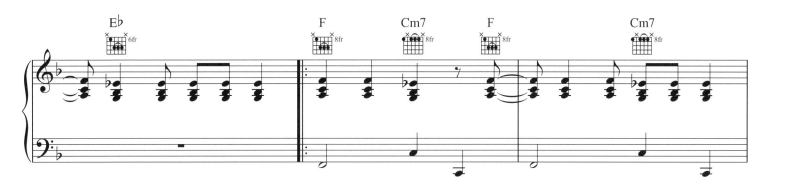

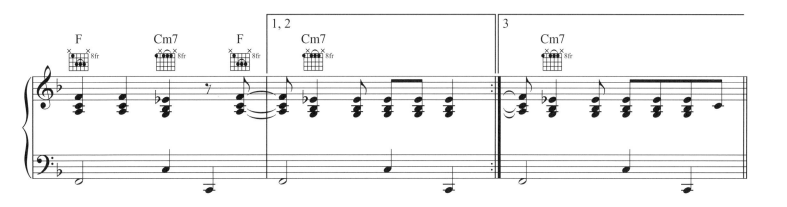

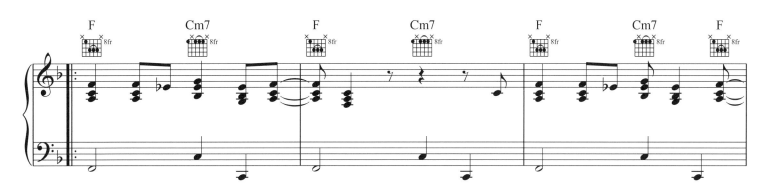

THAT'LL BE THE DAY

Words and Music by JERRY ALLISON,
NORMAN PETTY and BUDDY HOLLY

THAT'S AMORÉ
(That's Love)

Words by JACK BROOKS
Music by HARRY WARREN

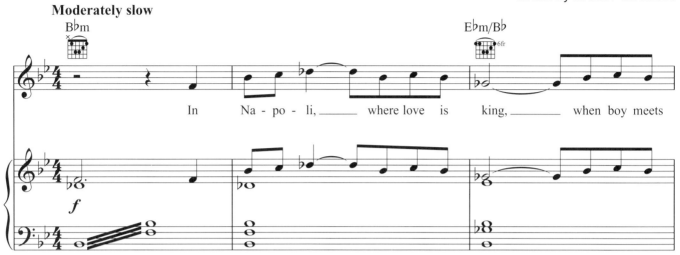

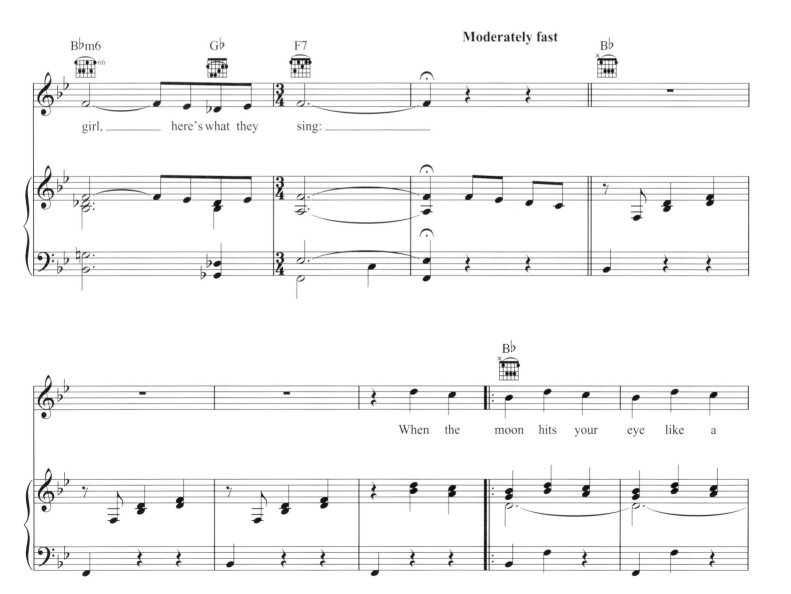

TOM DOOLEY

Words and Music Collected, Adapted and Arranged by
FRANK WARNER, JOHN A. LOMAX and ALAN LOMAX
From the singing of FRANK PROFFITT

Hang down your head, Tom Doo- ley, hang down your head and cry.

Hang down your head, Tom Doo- ley. Poor boy, you're bound _ to die. I

met her on the moun- tain, and there I took her life. I
This time to- mor- row, reck- on where I'll be?
This time to- mor- row, reck- on where I'll be? If it

TRUE LOVE

Words and Music by
COLE PORTER

TUTTI FRUTTI

Words and Music by LITTLE RICHARD PENNIMAN
and DOROTHY LA BOSTRIE

UNCHAINED MELODY

Lyric by HY ZARET
Music by ALEX NORTH

291

292

VOLARE

Music by DOMENICO MODUGNO
English Lyric by MITCHELL PARISH
Original Italian Text by DOMENICO MODUGNO
and FRANCESCO MIGLIACCI

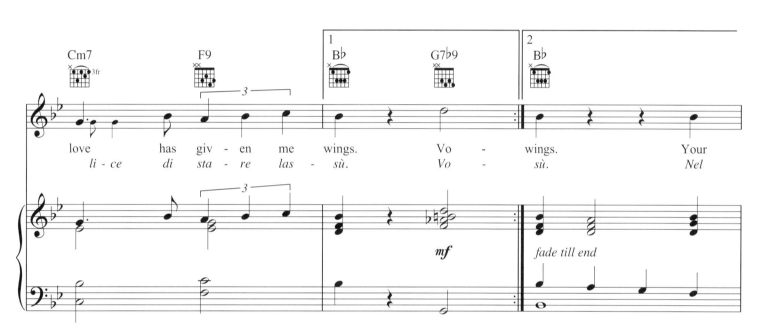

VENUS

Words and Music by
EDWARD MARSHALL

WAKE UP LITTLE SUSIE

Words and Music by BOUDLEAUX BRYANT
and FELICE BRYANT

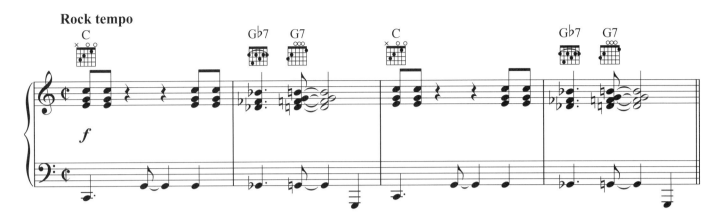

Wake up, Lit - tle Su - sie, ___ wake up.

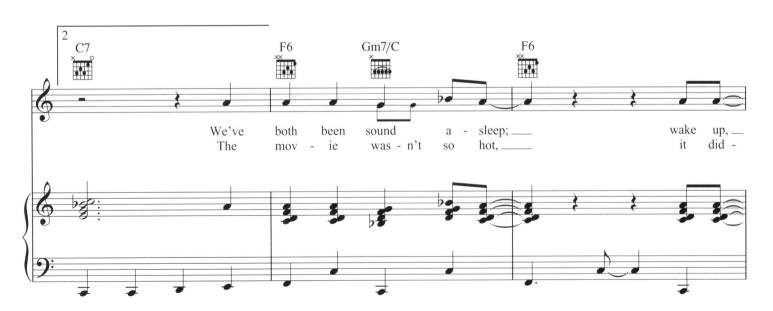

We've both been sound a - sleep; ___ wake up, ___
The mov - ie was - n't so hot, ___ it did -

THE WAYWARD WIND

Words and Music by HERB NEWMAN
and STAN LEBOWSKY

WHAT'D I SAY

Words and Music by
RAY CHARLES

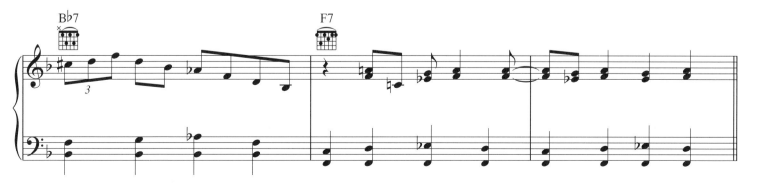

WEAR MY RING AROUND YOUR NECK

Words and Music by BERT CARROLL
and RUSSELL MOODY

F7 C C7
say that we're too young to know the mean - ing of a ring. I
F7 C
on - ly know I love ___ you and that you love me, too. So,
D7 G7 D7♭5 G7 N.C.
dar - ling, please do what I ask of you. ___ Won't you wear my
C
ring a - round your neck to tell the

A WHITE SPORT COAT
(And a Pink Carnation)

Words and Music by
MARTY ROBBINS

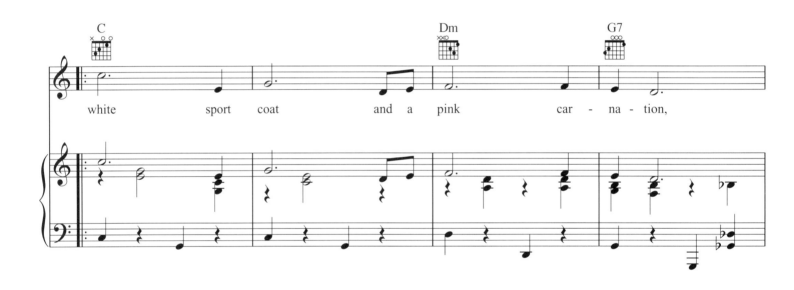

white sport coat and a pink car - na - tion,

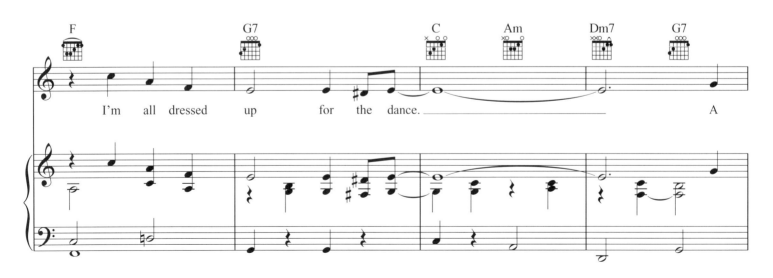

I'm all dressed up for the dance.

322

WHY DO FOOLS FALL IN LOVE

Words and Music by MORRIS LEVY
and FRANKIE LYMON

WHY DON'T YOU BELIEVE ME

Words and Music by LEW DOUGLAS,
LUTHER KING LANEY and LEROY W. RODDE

YOU SEND ME

Words and Music by
SAM COOKE

YAKETY YAK

Words and Music by JERRY LEIBER
and MIKE STOLLER

YOU BELONG TO ME

Words and Music by PEE WEE KING,
REDD STEWART and CHILTON PRICE

YOUNG LOVE

Words and Music by RIC CARTEY
and CAROLE JOYNER

F G7 C Am7 F G7
ev - er in my heart. Young
love for you or for me.
C G7 F G7
love, first love, filled with true de -
C Am7 F G7 C G7 F
vo - tion. Young love, our love we share with
1 2 D.S. and Fade
G7 C Am7 F G7 F G7
deep e - mo - tion. Young

YOUR CHEATIN' HEART

Words and Music by
HANK WILLIAMS